Table of Conten[ts]

This lesson plan book belongs to:

Name _____

School _____

Grade/Subject _____

Room _____

School Year _____

Address _____

Phone _____

Teacher Created Resources, Inc.
6421 Industry Way
Westminster, CA 92683
www.teachercreated.com
ISBN: 978-1-57690-122-9

©1999 Teacher Created Resources, Inc.
Reprinted, 2007
Made in U.S.A.

Editorial Project Manager: Ina Massler Levin
Cover Art: Denise Bauer
Imaging: Ralph Olmedo, Jr.

Ways to Use This Book

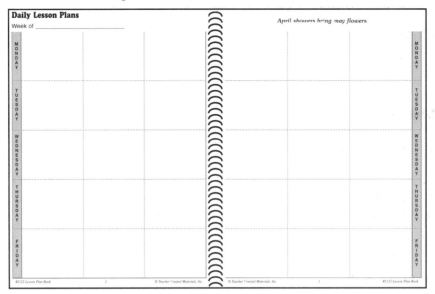

Seating Chart (page 3)

Table or desk arrangement will vary depending on room size, grade level, and actual teaching style preferred.

Suggestions have been given, but you may wish to customize your seating for the optimum learning benefits of your students.

Student Roster (pages 4 & 5)

Record both student and parent names and addresses. Make a special note of differences in last names when appropriate. You may wish to list siblings and their grades if they also attend your school. Notes may include special needs children and medications necessary.

Substitute Teacher Information (pages 6 & 7)

Record all pertinent information on these pages. If you have a copy of the layout of your school, attach it to this page; otherwise, sketch an outline of the school grounds, showing restrooms, office, lounge, playground, etc. Paper clip this page as well as the lesson plan page for easy reference.

Year at a Glance (page 8)

This section will give you an overview of the year and help focus on immediate and upcoming events, conferences, meetings, seminars, and other important dates. Record each event as soon as you are notified.

Birthdays (page 9)

Write names and birthdates of students in boxes. Identify each special day with a birthday greeting. With young children, sing to them and present them with a special birthday hat.

Emergency and First Aid Information (page 10)

Keep a First Aid Kit in an easy-to-find place and show the children where it is kept. During the first week of school you may wish to go over the listed emergency information with your children. In the blanks provided, list persons qualified to administer CPR along with their room numbers. Attach a list of school emergency procedures.

Literary Awards, Metric Conversions, States, Provinces and Capitals and World Map (pages 11–14)

These pages can be used as easy reference throughout the year. Also, you may wish to create puzzles and games using these fact pages.

Chalkboard Challenges (page 15)

These puzzles, games, and brain teasers will promote critical thinking for the students. They can be used as supplementary assignments, homework, or emergency substitute plans.

Daily Lesson Plans (pages 16-95)

Use the daily lesson plan pages to help you organize your lesson plans for the week. In the blank that says "Week of __" add the dates for the week. You may wish to use the last column for notes or evaluation.

Quote of the Week (pages 16-95)

Each weekly lesson plan page features a proverb which can be used as a quote for the week. Proverbs are sayings that have withstood the test of time. They are open to interpretation by students. These can be shared with students by copying them onto the chalkboard or by reading them aloud. Use these quotes to spark discussion, as journal topics, or to enhance critical thinking skills.

Seating Chart

Seat Arrangement Ideas

Sticky notes can be used to temporarily assign seats.

1. Basic Row Seating

2. U-Shaped Seating

3. Rectangle

4. Partner Seating

The size and shape of your room will play a large part in your seating arrangement.

You may want to change this layout once you are familiar with your students and their needs.

Regardless of your seating plan, the most important concern is that you can easily see all your students and the children in turn have good visibility of you, the chalkboard, and other focal points in the room.

Front of Classroom

Student Roster

	Student's Name	Parent's Name	Address
1.			
2.			
3.			
4.			
5.			
6.			
7.			
8.			
9.			
10.			
11.			
12.			
13.			
14.			
15.			
16.			
17.			
18.			
19.			
20.			
21.			
22.			
23.			
24.			
25.			
26.			
27.			
28.			
29.			
30.			
31.			
32.			
33.			
34.			
35.			
36.			

Student Roster *(cont.)*

Home & Work Phones	Birthday	Siblings	Notes

Substitute Teacher Information

School Schedule

- Class Begins_____
- Morning Recess_____
- Lunchtime _____
- Class Resumes_____
- Afternoon Recess_____
- Dismissal _____

Special Notes

_____
_____
_____
_____
_____
_____
_____
_____

Special Classes

Student _____

Class _____ Day _____ Time _____

Student _____

Class _____ Day _____ Time _____

Student _____

Class _____Day _____Time _____

Where to Find

- Class List _____
- School Layout _____
- Seating Chart _____
- Attendance Record_____
- Lesson Plans _____
- Teacher Manuals _____
- First Aid Kit _____
- Emergency Information _____
- Supplementary Activities _____
- Class Supplies–paper, pencils, etc _____
- Referral forms and procedures _____

_____
_____
_____
_____
_____
_____
_____
_____
_____
_____
_____

Special Needs Students

Student	Needs	Time and Place
_____	_____	_____
_____	_____	_____
_____	_____	_____
_____	_____	_____
_____	_____	_____

Substitute Teacher Information *(cont.)*

Classroom Standards

- When finished with an assignment

  _____

  _____

- When and how to speak out in class

  _____

  _____

- Incentive Program

  _____

  _____

- Discipline

  _____

  _____

- Restroom Procedure

  _____

  _____

People Who Can Help

- Teacher/Room_____

- Dependable Students _____

  _____

  _____

  _____

  _____

  _____

- Principal _____

- Secretary_____

- Custodian _____

- Counselor _____

- Nurse _____

Layout of School—including school office, teachers' lounge, restrooms, auditorium, playground, etc. (or attach printed diagram here)

Year at a Glance

August	September	October
_____	_____	_____
_____	_____	_____
_____	_____	_____
_____	_____	_____
_____	_____	_____
_____		_____

November	December	January
_____	_____	_____
_____	_____	_____
_____	_____	_____
_____	_____	_____
_____	_____	_____
	_____	

February	March	April
_____	_____	_____
_____	_____	_____
_____	_____	_____
_____	_____	_____
_____	_____	_____

May	June	July
_____	_____	_____
_____	_____	_____
_____	_____	_____
_____	_____	_____
	_____	

Birthdays

August	September	October
_____	_____	_____
_____	_____	_____
_____	_____	_____
_____	_____	_____
_____	_____	_____

November	December	January
_____	_____	_____
_____	_____	_____
_____	_____	_____
_____	_____	_____
_____	_____	_____

February	March	April
_____	_____	_____
_____	_____	_____
_____	_____	_____
_____	_____	_____
_____	_____	_____

May	June	July
_____	_____	_____
_____	_____	_____
_____	_____	_____
_____	_____	_____
_____	_____	_____

Emergency and First Aid Information

Classroom Caution

- Do not move a person who is seriously injured.
- Report all head injuries to the nurse or office.
- Show children where the first aid kit is stored.
- List students with medical problems and any medications.
- Instruct children about nose blowing and covering their mouths when coughing and sneezing.
- Inform students about what to do if they feel they are going to be ill.
- The best way to stop bleeding is to put pressure on the wound.

  a. Use a clean pad, a cloth, a plastic bag, or any other object that will keep you from touching the blood directly. (Never allow the blood to touch your skin.)

  b. Place your hand over the pad or cloth, pressing firmly and steadily until the bleeding stops or someone comes to help.

  c. Do not remove the pad or cloth. You might start the bleeding again. Instead, add more pads or cloth and keep pressing.

  d. If the part that is bleeding can be raised higher than the victim's head, do so; this will slow down the flow of blood.

  e. Keep the victim from moving—especially the wounded area.

First Aid for Choking
Adults/Children

If conscious but *choking*...

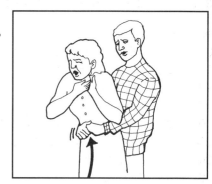

Give abdominal thrusts until object comes out.

If person becomes *unconscious*...

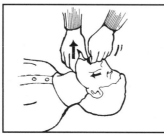

Step 1
Clear any object from the mouth.

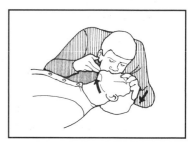

Step 2
Give two slow breaths.

If air won't go in...

Step 3
Give up to five abdominal thrusts.

Repeat steps 1, 2, & 3 until breaths go in or help arrives.

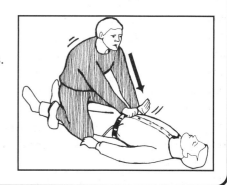

Trained CPR person at our school:

Name _____ Room _____

Name _____ Room _____

Name _____ Room _____

Name _____ Room _____

Name _____ Room _____

Name _____ Room _____

Name _____ Room _____

Newbery and Caldecott Awards

The Newbery Medal is awarded each year to the author of the most distinguished contribution to children's literature published in the United States. Here are the winners from 1960 to 2000.

Year	Title/Author
2000	*Bud, Not Buddy.* by Christopher Paul Curtis
1999	*Holes.* by Louis Sachar
1998	*Out of The Dust.* Karen Hesse
1997	*The View From Saturday.* E.L. Konigsburg
1996	*Midwife's Apprentice.* Karen Cushman
1995	*Walk Two Moons.* Sharon Creech
1994	*The Giver.* Lois Lowry
1993	*Missing May.* Cynthia Rylant
1992	*Shiloh.* Phyllis Reynolds
1991	*Maniac Magee.* Jerry Spinelli
1990	*Number the Stars.* Lois Lowry
1989	*Joyful Noise.* Paul Fleischman
1988	*Lincoln: A Photobiography.* Russell Freedman
1987	*The Whipping Boy.* Sid Fleischman
1986	*Sarah, Plain and Tall.* Patricia MacLachlan
1985	*The Hero and the Crown.* Robin McKinly
1984	*Dear Mr. Henshaw.* Beverly Cleary
1983	*Dicey's Song.* Cynthia Voigt
1982	*A Visit to William Blake's Inn.* Nancy Willard
1981	*Jacob Have I Loved.* Katherine Paterson
1980	*A Gathering of Days.* Joan W. Blos
1979	*The Westing Game.* Ellen Raskin
1978	*Bridge to Terabithia.* Katherine Paterson
1977	*Roll of Thunder, Hear My Cry.* Mildred Taylor
1976	*The Grey King.* Susan Cooper
1975	*M.C. Higgins, the Great.* Virginia Hamilton
1974	*The Slave Dancer.* Paula Fox
1973	*Julie of the Wolves.* Jean George
1972	*Mrs. Frisby and the Rats of NIMH.* Robert C. O'Brien
1971	*Summer of the Swans.* Betsy Byars
1970	*Sounder.* William H. Armstrong
1969	*The High King.* Lloyd Alexander
1968	*From the Mixed-Up Files of Mrs. Basil E. Frankweiler.* E.L. Konigsburg
1967	*Up a Road Slowly.* Irene Hunt
1966	*I, Juan de Pareja.* Elizabeth Borton de Trevino
1965	*Shadow of a Bull.* Maia Wojciechowska
1964	*It's Like This, Cat.* Emily C. Neville
1963	*A Wrinkle in Time.* Madeline L'Engle
1962	*The Bronze Bow.* Elizabeth C. Speare
1961	*Island of the Blue Dolphins.* Scott O'Dell
1960	*Onion John.* Joseph Krumgold

The Caldecott Medal is presented to the illustrator of the most distinguished picture book for children published in the United States. Here are the winners from 1960 to 2000.

Year	Title/Illustrator
2000	*Joseph Had a Little Overcoat.* by Simms Taback
1999	*Snowflake Bentley.* by Mary Azarian
1998	*Rapunzel.* by Paul O. Zelinsky
1997	*Golem.* David Wishiewski
1996	*Officer Buckle and Gloria.* P. Rathmann
1995	*Smoky Night.* David Diaz
1994	*Grandfather's Journey.* Allen Say
1993	*Mirette on the High Wire.* Emily A. McCully
1992	*Tuesday.* David Wiesner
1991	*Black and White.* David Macaulay
1990	*Lon Po Po.* Ed Young
1989	*Song and Dance Man.* Stephen Gammell
1988	*Owl Moon.* John Schoenherr
1987	*Hey, Al.* Richard Egielski
1986	*The Polar Express.* Chris Van Allsburg
1985	*Saint George and the Dragon.* Trina Schart Hyman
1984	*The Glorious Flight: Across the Channel with Louis Bleriot.* Alice and Martin Provensen
1983	*Shadow.* Marcia Brown
1982	*Jumanji.* Chris Van Allsburg
1981	*Fables.* Arnold Lobel
1980	*Ox-Cart Man.* Barbara Cooney
1979	*The Girl Who Loved Wild Horses.* Paul Goble
1978	*Noah's Ark.* Peter Spier
1977	*Ashanti to Zulu: African Traditions.* Leo and Diane Dillon
1976	*Why Mosquitoes Buzz in People's Ears.* Leo and Diane Dillon
1975	*Arrow to the Sun: A Pueblo Indian Tale.* Gerald McDermott
1974	*Duffy and the Devil.* Margot Zemach
1973	*The Funny Little Woman.* Blair Lent
1972	*One Fine Day.* Nonny Hogrogian
1971	*A Story, A Story.* Gail E. Haley
1970	*Sylvester and the Magic Pebble.* William Steig
1969	*The Fool of the World and the Flying Ship.* Uri Shulevitz
1968	*Drummer Hoff.* Ed Emberley
1967	*Sam, Bangs and Moonshine.* Evaline Ness
1966	*Always Room for One More.* Nonny Hogrogian
1965	*May I Bring a Friend?* Beni Montresor
1964	*Where the Wild Things Are.* Maurice Sendak
1963	*The Snowy Day.* Ezra Jack Keats
1962	*Once a Mouse.* Marcia Brown
1961	*Baboushka and the Three Kings.* Nicolas Sidjakov
1960	*Nine Days to Christmas.* Marie Hall Ets

Metric Conversions

Linear

100 cm	=	1 meter
cm	=	centimeter
¼"	=	.6 cm
½"	=	1.3 cm
1"	=	2.54 cm
3"	=	7.62 cm
6"	=	15.24 cm
9"	=	22.86 cm
12"	=	30.48 cm
18"	=	45.72 cm
24"	=	61 cm
36"	=	91.44 cm
100 yds	=	91.4 m
1 mile	=	1,609 m

Volume (dry and liquid)

L	=	liter
mL	=	milliliter = .001 L
1 tsp	=	5 mL
1 T	=	15 mL
¼ c	=	59 mL
½ c	=	118 mL
1 c	=	236 mL or 8 oz. = .236 L
1 oz	=	30 mL
1 pt	=	about .5 L (473.2 mL)
1 qt	=	about 1 L (946.4 mL)
1 gal	=	about 3.8 L
1 L	=	1.0567 qts liquid
1 qt dry	=	1.101 L
1 qt liquid	=	.09463 L
1 gal liquid	=	3.78541 L

Temperatures

To convert Fahrenheit to Celsius (F° - 32 x .55)
To convert Celsius to Fahrenheit (C° x 1.8) + 32

	Celsius	Fahrenheit
boiling point of water	100°	212°
freezing point of water	0°	32°
cold day	-20°	-4°
room temperature	20°	66°
body temperature	37°	98.6°

Oven Temperatures

	Celsius	Fahrenheit
warm oven	135°	275°
moderate oven	175°	350°
hot oven	204°	400°

Weights

1 gram	=	0.03527 ounce
1 ounce	=	28.35 gram
1 kilogram	=	2.2046 lbs
1 pound	=	453.4 gram or .454 kilogram
1 ton	=	908 kilograms

States, Provinces and Capitals

UNITED STATES

State	Capital
Alabama	Montgomery
Alaska	Juneau
Arizona	Phoenix
Arkansas	Little Rock
California	Sacramento
Colorado	Denver
Connecticut	Hartford
Delaware	Dover
Florida	Tallahassee
Georgia	Atlanta
Hawaii	Honolulu
Idaho	Boise
Illinois	Springfield
Indiana	Indianapolis
Iowa	Des Moines
Kansas	Topeka
Kentucky	Frankfort
Louisiana	Baton Rouge
Maine	Augusta
Maryland	Annapolis
Massachusetts	Boston
Michigan	Lansing
Minnesota	St. Paul
Mississippi	Jackson
Missouri	Jefferson City
Montana	Helena
Nebraska	Lincoln
Nevada	Carson City
New Hampshire	Concord
New Jersey	Trenton
New Mexico	Santa Fe
New York	Albany
North Carolina	Raleigh
North Dakota	Bismarck
Ohio	Columbus
Oklahoma	Oklahoma City
Oregon	Salem
Pennsylvania	Harrisburg
Rhode Island	Providence
South Carolina	Columbia
South Dakota	Pierre
Tennessee	Nashville
Texas	Austin
Utah	Salt Lake City
Vermont	Montpelier
Virginia	Richmond
Washington	Olympia
West Virginia	Charleston
Wisconsin	Madison
Wyoming	Cheyenne
Nation's Capital	Washington, D.C.

CANADA

Province	Capital
Alberta	Edmonton
British Columbia	Victoria
Manitoba	Winnipeg
New Brunswick	Fredericton
Newfoundland	St. John's
Nova Scotia	Halifax
Ontario	Toronto
Prince Edward Island	Charlottetown
Quebec	Quebec
Saskatchewan	Regina

Territories

	Capital
Northwest Territories	Yellowknife
Yukon Territory	Whitehorse

MEXICO

State	Capital
Aguascalientes	Aguascalientes
Baja California Norte	Mexicali
Baja California Sur	La Paz
Campeche	Campeche
Chiapas	Tuxtla Gutierrez
Chihuahua	Chihuahua
Coahuila	Saltillo
Colima	Colima
Durango	Durango
Federal District	—
Guanajuato	Guanajuato
Guerrero	Chilpancingo
Hidalgo	Pachuca
Jalisco	Guadalajara
México	Toluca
Michoacán	Morelia
Morelos	Cuernavaca
Nayarit	Tepic
Nuevo León	Monterrey
Oaxaca	Oaxaca
Puebla	Puebla
Querétaro	Querétaro
Quintana Roo	Chetumal
San Luis Potosí	San Luis Potosí
Sinaloa	Culiacán
Sonora	Hermosillo
Tabasco	Villahermosa
Tamaulipas	Ciudad Victoria
Tlaxcala	Tlaxcala
Veracruz	Jalapa
Yucatán	Mérida
Zacatecas	Zacatecas

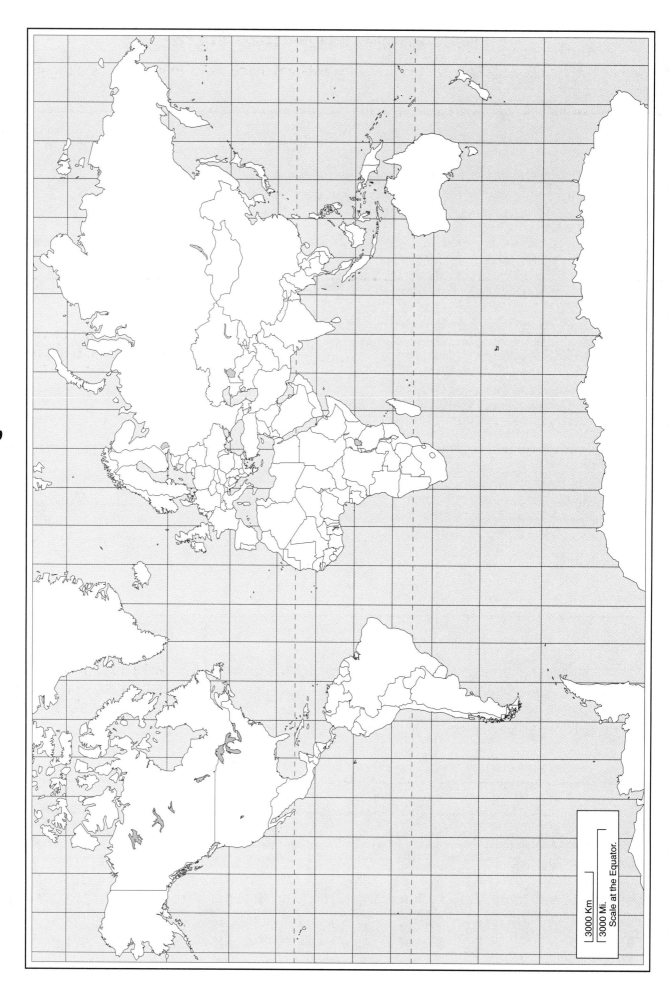

World Map

3000 Km
3000 Mi.
Scale at the Equator.

14

From little acorns mighty oaks do grow.

			MONDAY
			TUESDAY
			WEDNESDAY
			THURSDAY
			FRIDAY

Daily Lesson Plans

Week of _____

MONDAY			
TUESDAY			
WEDNESDAY			
THURSDAY			
FRIDAY			

Actions speak louder than words.

			MONDAY
			TUESDAY
			WEDNESDAY
			THURSDAY
			FRIDAY

Daily Lesson Plans

Week of _____

MONDAY			
TUESDAY			
WEDNESDAY			
THURSDAY			
FRIDAY			

All that glitters is not gold.

			MONDAY
			TUESDAY
			WEDNESDAY
			THURSDAY
			FRIDAY

Daily Lesson Plans

Week of _____

MONDAY			
TUESDAY			
WEDNESDAY			
THURSDAY			
FRIDAY			

April showers bring May flowers.

			MONDAY
			TUESDAY
			WEDNESDAY
			THURSDAY
			FRIDAY

Daily Lesson Plans

Week of _____

MONDAY			
TUESDAY			
WEDNESDAY			
THURSDAY			
FRIDAY			

Beauty is only skin deep.

			MONDAY
			TUESDAY
			WEDNESDAY
			THURSDAY
			FRIDAY

Daily Lesson Plans

Week of _____

MONDAY			
TUESDAY			
WEDNESDAY			
THURSDAY			
FRIDAY			

Don't put the cart before the horse.

			MONDAY
			TUESDAY
			WEDNESDAY
			THURSDAY
			FRIDAY

Daily Lesson Plans

Week of _____

MONDAY			
TUESDAY			
WEDNESDAY			
THURSDAY			
FRIDAY			

Don't count your chickens before they hatch.

			MONDAY
			TUESDAY
			WEDNESDAY
			THURSDAY
			FRIDAY

Daily Lesson Plans

Week of _____

MONDAY			
TUESDAY			
WEDNESDAY			
THURSDAY			
FRIDAY			

Don't cry over spilt milk.

			MONDAY
			TUESDAY
			WEDNESDAY
			THURSDAY
			FRIDAY

Daily Lesson Plans

Week of _____

MONDAY			
TUESDAY			
WEDNESDAY			
THURSDAY			
FRIDAY			

The early bird catches the worm.

			MONDAY
			TUESDAY
			WEDNESDAY
			THURSDAY
			FRIDAY

Daily Lesson Plans

Week of _____

MONDAY			
TUESDAY			
WEDNESDAY			
THURSDAY			
FRIDAY			

You can catch more flies with honey than with vinegar.

			MONDAY
			TUESDAY
			WEDNESDAY
			THURSDAY
			FRIDAY

Daily Lesson Plans

Week of _____

MONDAY			
TUESDAY			
WEDNESDAY			
THURSDAY			
FRIDAY			

A friend in need is a friend indeed.

			MONDAY
			TUESDAY
			WEDNESDAY
			THURSDAY
			FRIDAY

Daily Lesson Plans

Week of _____

MONDAY			
TUESDAY			
WEDNESDAY			
THURSDAY			
FRIDAY			

Genius is one percent inspiration and ninety-nine percent perspiration.

			MONDAY
			TUESDAY
			WEDNESDAY
			THURSDAY
			FRIDAY

Daily Lesson Plans

Week of _____

MONDAY			
TUESDAY			
WEDNESDAY			
THURSDAY			
FRIDAY			

The grass is always greener on the other side of the fence.

			MONDAY
			TUESDAY
			WEDNESDAY
			THURSDAY
			FRIDAY

Daily Lesson Plans

Week of _____

MONDAY			
TUESDAY			
WEDNESDAY			
THURSDAY			
FRIDAY			

Haste makes waste.

			MONDAY
			TUESDAY
			WEDNESDAY
			THURSDAY
			FRIDAY

Daily Lesson Plans

Week of _____

MONDAY			
TUESDAY			
WEDNESDAY			
THURSDAY			
FRIDAY			

Here today, gone tomorrow.

			MONDAY
			TUESDAY
			WEDNESDAY
			THURSDAY
			FRIDAY

Daily Lesson Plans

Week of _____

MONDAY			
TUESDAY			
WEDNESDAY			
THURSDAY			
FRIDAY			

Hitch your wagon to a star.

			MONDAY
			TUESDAY
			WEDNESDAY
			THURSDAY
			FRIDAY

Daily Lesson Plans

Week of _____

MONDAY			
TUESDAY			
WEDNESDAY			
THURSDAY			
FRIDAY			

Imitation is the sincerest form of flattery.

			MONDAY
			TUESDAY
			WEDNESDAY
			THURSDAY
			FRIDAY

Daily Lesson Plans

Week of _____

MONDAY			
TUESDAY			
WEDNESDAY			
THURSDAY			
FRIDAY			

Knowledge is power.

			MONDAY
			TUESDAY
			WEDNESDAY
			THURSDAY
			FRIDAY

Daily Lesson Plans

Week of _____

MONDAY			
TUESDAY			
WEDNESDAY			
THURSDAY			
FRIDAY			

Look before you leap.

			MONDAY
			TUESDAY
			WEDNESDAY
			THURSDAY
			FRIDAY

Daily Lesson Plans

Week of _____

MONDAY			
TUESDAY			
WEDNESDAY			
THURSDAY			
FRIDAY			

Love makes the world go 'round.

			MONDAY
			TUESDAY
			WEDNESDAY
			THURSDAY
			FRIDAY

Daily Lesson Plans

Week of _____

MONDAY			
TUESDAY			
WEDNESDAY			
THURSDAY			
FRIDAY			

Make haste slowly.

			MONDAY
			TUESDAY
			WEDNESDAY
			THURSDAY
			FRIDAY

Daily Lesson Plans

Week of _____

MONDAY			
TUESDAY			
WEDNESDAY			
THURSDAY			
FRIDAY			

Make hay while the sun shines.

			MONDAY
			TUESDAY
			WEDNESDAY
			THURSDAY
			FRIDAY

Daily Lesson Plans

Week of _____

MONDAY			
TUESDAY			
WEDNESDAY			
THURSDAY			
FRIDAY			

Many hands make light work.

			MONDAY
			TUESDAY
			WEDNESDAY
			THURSDAY
			FRIDAY

Daily Lesson Plans

Week of _____

MONDAY			
TUESDAY			
WEDNESDAY			
THURSDAY			
FRIDAY			

Never put off until tomorrow what you can do today.

			MONDAY
			TUESDAY
			WEDNESDAY
			THURSDAY
			FRIDAY

Daily Lesson Plans

Week of _____

M O N D A Y			
T U E S D A Y			
W E D N E S D A Y			
T H U R S D A Y			
F R I D A Y			

Nothing succeeds like success.

			MONDAY
			TUESDAY
			WEDNESDAY
			THURSDAY
			FRIDAY

Daily Lesson Plans

Week of _____

MONDAY			
TUESDAY			
WEDNESDAY			
THURSDAY			
FRIDAY			

One picture is worth a thousand words.

			MONDAY
			TUESDAY
			WEDNESDAY
			THURSDAY
			FRIDAY

Daily Lesson Plans

Week of _____

MONDAY			
TUESDAY			
WEDNESDAY			
THURSDAY			
FRIDAY			

One rotten apple spoils the barrel.

			MONDAY
			TUESDAY
			WEDNESDAY
			THURSDAY
			FRIDAY

Daily Lesson Plans

Week of _____

MONDAY			
TUESDAY			
WEDNESDAY			
THURSDAY			
FRIDAY			

The pen is mightier than the sword.

			MONDAY
			TUESDAY
			WEDNESDAY
			THURSDAY
			FRIDAY

Daily Lesson Plans

Week of _____

MONDAY			
TUESDAY			
WEDNESDAY			
THURSDAY			
FRIDAY			

A penny saved is a penny earned.

			MONDAY
			TUESDAY
			WEDNESDAY
			THURSDAY
			FRIDAY

Daily Lesson Plans

Week of _____

M O N D A Y			
T U E S D A Y			
W E D N E S D A Y			
T H U R S D A Y			
F R I D A Y			

Practice makes perfect.

			MONDAY
			TUESDAY
			WEDNESDAY
			THURSDAY
			FRIDAY

Daily Lesson Plans

Week of _____

MONDAY			
TUESDAY			
WEDNESDAY			
THURSDAY			
FRIDAY			

Rome wasn't built in a day.

			MONDAY
			TUESDAY
			WEDNESDAY
			THURSDAY
			FRIDAY

Daily Lesson Plans

Week of _____

MONDAY			
TUESDAY			
WEDNESDAY			
THURSDAY			
FRIDAY			

Silence is golden.

			MONDAY
			TUESDAY
			WEDNESDAY
			THURSDAY
			FRIDAY

Daily Lesson Plans

Week of _____

MONDAY			
TUESDAY			
WEDNESDAY			
THURSDAY			
FRIDAY			

A stitch in time saves nine.

			MONDAY
			TUESDAY
			WEDNESDAY
			THURSDAY
			FRIDAY

Daily Lesson Plans

Week of _____

MONDAY			
TUESDAY			
WEDNESDAY			
THURSDAY			
FRIDAY			

Don't throw out the baby with the bath water.

			MONDAY
			TUESDAY
			WEDNESDAY
			THURSDAY
			FRIDAY

Daily Lesson Plans

Week of _____

MONDAY			
TUESDAY			
WEDNESDAY			
THURSDAY			
FRIDAY			

Truth will out.

			MONDAY
			TUESDAY
			WEDNESDAY
			THURSDAY
			FRIDAY

Daily Lesson Plans

Week of _____

MONDAY			
TUESDAY			
WEDNESDAY			
THURSDAY			
FRIDAY			

A watched pot never boils.

			MONDAY
			TUESDAY
			WEDNESDAY
			THURSDAY
			FRIDAY

Daily Lesson Plans

Week of _____

MONDAY			
TUESDAY			
WEDNESDAY			
THURSDAY			
FRIDAY			

Where there's a will, there's a way.

			MONDAY
			TUESDAY
			WEDNESDAY
			THURSDAY
			FRIDAY

Daily Lesson Plans

Week of _____

MONDAY			
TUESDAY			
WEDNESDAY			
THURSDAY			
FRIDAY			

A word to the wise is sufficient.

			MONDAY
			TUESDAY
			WEDNESDAY
			THURSDAY
			FRIDAY

Daily Lesson Plans

Week of _____

MONDAY			
TUESDAY			
WEDNESDAY			
THURSDAY			
FRIDAY			

If the shoe fits, wear it.

			MONDAY
			TUESDAY
			WEDNESDAY
			THURSDAY
			FRIDAY

Notes